Contents

Chapter 1
Using a Template

What is Microsoft PowerPoint?

Microsoft PowerPoint is the leading graphics presentation package. You can use it to create, design and organise professional presentations quickly and easily. You can then:

 give the presentation yourself

 set it to run automatically on its own or

 let users use it as an interactive Web style system with links to different pages of the presentation

Getting started

 Load Microsoft PowerPoint. You can do this in one of two ways:

 Either double-click the **PowerPoint** icon

 Or click **Start** at the bottom left of the screen, then click **Programs**, Microsoft PowerPoint on the menu.

Your screen will look like this:

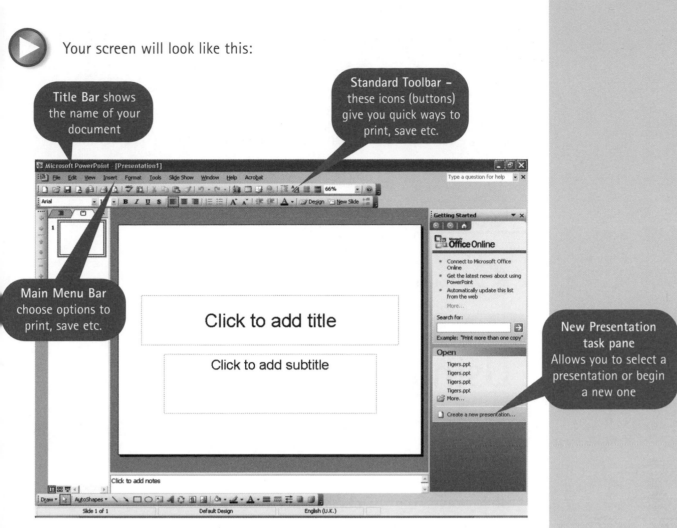

Figure 1.1: The opening screen

Over the next several chapters you'll be working on a presentation of several slides. This will be of the sort that you would deliver yourself to an audience or have automatically running for people to look at in their own time.

Planning a presentation

To deliver an effective presentation you need to consider who your audience is, and prepare your slides to suit them. The audience could be your classmates, your teachers or even the general public once you are working for a real company.

Whoever your presentation is for, here are a few basic guidelines:

 Start with a title screen showing what the project is about.

 Don't put more than 4 or 5 points on each slide. People can't concentrate on too much information at once.

 Keep each point short and simple. You may want to talk around each point to explain it in further detail.

 Sound, graphics and animation can add interest, but don't overdo them!

Using a Template

A quick way to create a colourful presentation is to use a Design Template.

Once PowerPoint is loaded, click **File**, **New**. You should see the New Presentation task pane on the right-hand side of the screen.

Tip:

The task pane will change depending on what task you are performing.

Figure 1.2: Selecting a Template

 Under the heading **New** select From Design Template (General Templates... in PowerPoint 2002.)

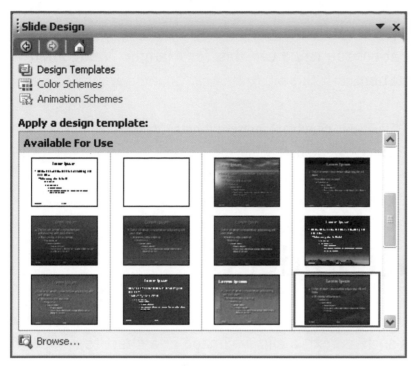

Figure 1.3: The Design Templates pane and selected design

Double-click the **Maple** template.

Click the down-arrow at the top of the **Slide Design** task pane and select **Slide Layout**.

In the **Slide Layout** task pane choose the first layout from the **Text Layouts** selection. This is a **Title Slide** and the most suitable layout for the first page of your new presentation.

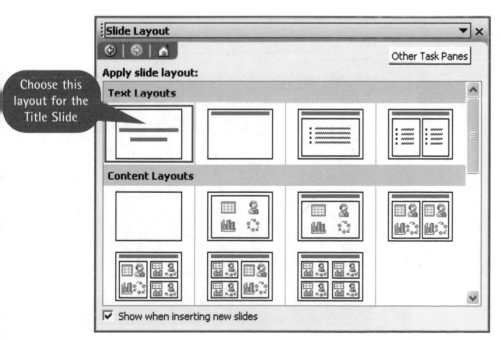

Figure 1.4: Various layout options

Close the **Slide Layout** task pane by clicking the X in its top right-hand corner.

You may want to make a new folder in which to save your presentation. You could call this, for example, **ValdeSoleil Presentation**.

 Save your new blank presentation as **ValdeSoleil.ppt** in the appropriate folder.

Val de Soleil is French for Sun Valley.

Placeholders

Each slide layout displays **placeholders** that allow you to easily add objects such as text, a clip art image or a chart to a slide. You will see two examples of these on the Title Slide, one for the title and another for the subtitle.

Adding text to the title screen

 Click the **Title** placeholder (where **PowerPoint** tells you to click) and type the title **Val de Soleil Resort**.

 Now add a sub-title. Click where indicated, and type: **Activities and Entertainment provided all year round**.

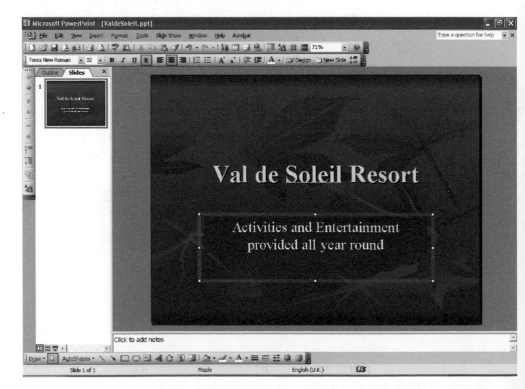

Figure 1.5: Adding text to your title screen

Formatting and moving the text

You can click the text boxes to move them around the screen. You can also format the text in each text box – for example, change its colour, size or alignment.

To format text you need to select the text box by clicking its border. When the border has changed from a diagonally striped box to a fuzzy one you know you can start formatting the text.

If you want to edit, add or delete text in a box, click inside the box. The border changes to diagonal stripes.

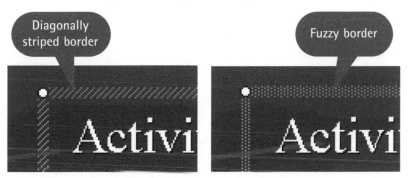

Figure 1.6: Formatting box pattern

▶ Select the fuzzy border around the sub-title text box.

▶ Make the text Italic by clicking on the **Italic** button. ────────── *I*

▶ Increase the font size to size 40. ──────────

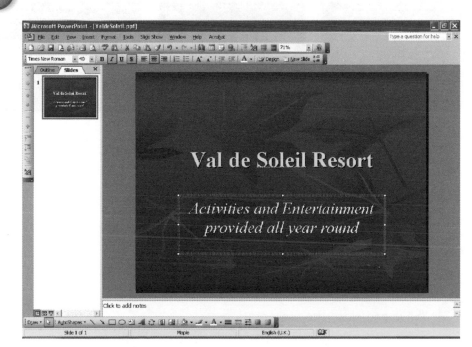

Figure 1.7: The title screen in Normal view

Tip:

If the **Italic** button is not visible, click the Toolbar Options button.

Then select **Show Buttons on Two Rows.**

Changing the view

You can alternate between various views of the presentation by clicking on the icons at the bottom of the screen.

Normal view

This is the most useful view as it lets you see, down the left of the screen, miniatures of each slide in your presentation. This is the view currently selected and shown in Figure 1.7.

Slide Sorter view

This view helps you to organise your slides in later stages. We'll be looking at this view later when you have more than one slide. Here's a preview of what it will look like when you have 6 slides:

Figure 1.8: Slide Sorter view

Slide Show view

Click this icon to view your presentation.

Save and close the presentation.

Tip:

You will be returned to the previously selected view after the last slide has been shown. You can press **Escape** (the key marked **Esc**) at any time during a presentation to end it.

8

Chapter 2

Editing a show

In this chapter you'll add some more to the presentation you started in Chapter 1. You will also learn how to change the order of your bullet points and swap the slides around.

Opening an existing presentation

▶ Load **PowerPoint** if it is not already open.

▶ Click **File, Open** to open the **ValdeSoleil.ppt** file you have been working on.

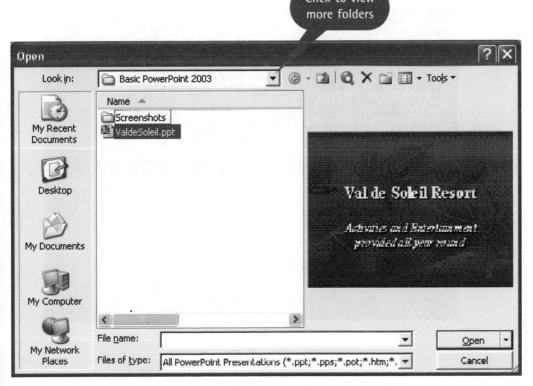

Figure 2.1: Opening an existing presentation

Tip:

Another way to open an existing presentation is click its name in the task pane. If the task pane is not open, it can be opened by selecting **Task Pane** from the **View** menu.

If you cannot see your filename, you can click the small downward arrow in the **Look In:** box as shown in Figure 2.1. This will bring up a list of folders for you to search.

 Make sure that you are in **Normal** View by clicking the **Normal view** button at the bottom of the screen.

Starting a new slide

Now you can begin the second slide of the presentation.

 Click the **New Slide** icon on the **Standard** toolbar.

The third layout, **Title and Text** is already selected for you by **PowerPoint** in the **Slide Layout** pane.

 Close the **Slide Layout** pane by clicking the small x in the top right of the pane. It will reappear each time you add another slide.

Enter the text as on the following screenshot, remembering to press **Enter** each time you need to start a new bullet point.

Note:

If you want to keep the **Slide Layout** task pane from displaying each time you click **New Slide**, clear the **Show when inserting new slides** check box at the bottom of the pane.

Leave it selected for now.

Sports and Entertainment

- Winter Sports
- Summer Sports
- Air Adventures
- Entertainment

Figure 2.2: Slide 2

Changing text size

You can increase or decrease the size of the text by using the **Font Size** button on the **Formatting** toolbar. PowerPoint also has special buttons for shrinking or enlarging the font one size at a time.

 Select all of the bulleted text on the current slide. (Alternatively, you can click in the text and then click the border around that placeholder.)

 Click several times on the **Increase Font Size** button to increase the size of the text. The button is located towards the right-hand end of the Formatting toolbar.

Your screen should now look something like Figure 2.3. (The text in this screen has been enlarged five times to size 54.)

Figure 2.3: Increasing the size of the text

Checking your spelling

You can check your spelling *either* by using the Main menu commands or by clicking the **Spelling and Grammar** button, which you will now do.

Click the **Spelling and Grammar** button on the left of the **Standard** toolbar.

PowerPoint will try to correct all the words it has underlined in red. It should find **Soleil**. Don't change this to **Solely**! Click **Ignore**.

Close the dialogue box.

Adding more slides

The next four slides are going to show more detail about each of the four activities available. New slides will be added after the current slide, so you need to be on your second slide.

Click the **New Slide** icon on the **Standard** toolbar.

Select the **Title and Text** layout as before and close the **New Slide** task pane.

Click the **Outline** tab at the top of the left-hand pane.

Type **Winter Sports** as the third slide title in the **Outline** pane. Press **Enter**.

A new slide should appear.

Type in the next 3 more slide titles, **Summer Sports**, **Air Adventures**, **Entertainment**, pressing **Enter** between each one.

Tip:

This is another way of adding a new slide.

You should now have four new slides, each with their own headings as shown in the Outline pane below.

1 Val de Soleil Resort
   Activities and Entertainment provided all year round

2 Sports and Entertainment
   • Winter Sports
   • Summer Sports
   • Air Adventures
   • Entertainment

3 Winter Sports

4 Summer Sports

5 Air Adventures

6 Entertainment

Figure 2.4

▶ Select the third slide by clicking its Slide icon. ———————  3

▶ Add text to this slide. Type Piste Hours from 08:30 – 16:00 where indicated on the slide and press Enter.

▶ Now press the Tab key or click the Increase Indent button to indent the next point.

The Increase/Decrease indent buttons

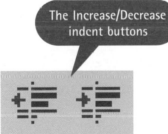

Tip:

If you are ever unsure about what a button does, hold your mouse pointer over it for a second and a **Tool Tip** will appear telling you what the button is called.

Your screen should now look like this:

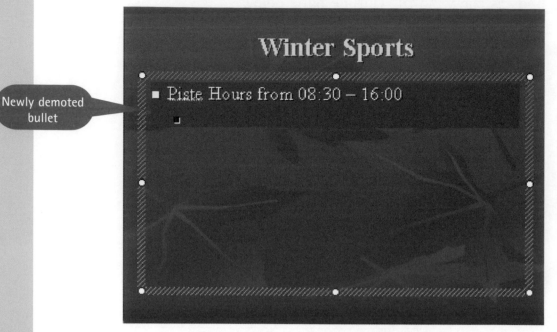

Figure 2.5: Demoting a new bullet point

Customising bullets

You can change the style and colour of bullets to increase the impact of a subset of points.

 Click the new line and select **Format**, **Bullets and Numbering...** on the menu.

 With the **Bulleted** tab selected, click **Customize...** in the bottom right corner of the window.

 The **Symbol** window will appear. Select a new shape for your bullet. Click **OK**.

Figure 2.6: Changing the appearance of bullets

This will only affect the style of bullets on this slide. To change the style of bullets throughout the entire presentation you should use the menu option **View, Master, Slide Master**. (See Chapter 7.) You can experiment with this later in your own presentations!

Note:

▶ Click **OK** again to close the Bullets and Numbering window.

▶ Underneath the **Piste Hours...** heading, type **Skiing** and then press **Enter**.

▶ Press the **Tab** key or click the **Increase Indent** button to indent the next point.

▶ Type in the next three lines as shown in Figure 2.7.

▶ Click the **Decrease Indent** button before typing **Snowboarding** Press **Enter**.

▶ Click the **Increase Indent** button again and then type the rest of the text as shown.

Winter Sports

Level 1 ■ **Piste Hours from 08:30 – 16:00**
Level 2 □ Skiing
Level 3 □ Lessons available from €15/hour
□ Night Skiing open Thursdays on Lower Slopes
□ Board Park open everyday
□ Snowboarding
□ Lessons available from €20/hour

Figure 2.7: Demoting bullet points – Levels 1, 2 and 3

Tip:

To get the **€** symbol press **Alt Gr** and **4** at the same time. (Alt Gr is on the right of the space bar.) Don't use the numeric keypad when pressing 4 – use the one on the main keyboard under the $ sign.

Moving text lines around

The Skiing feature, **Board Park...** should really be under the **Snowboarding** heading. Move this sentence down to its new place as follows:

 In the **Outline** pane on the left of the screen, click the mouse pointer to the left of **Board Park open everyday**. You will see a four-headed arrow style pointer.

Hold the left mouse button down and begin to drag downwards. A line will appear across the text. Keep going down until the line is underneath **Lessons available from €20/hour** and let go.

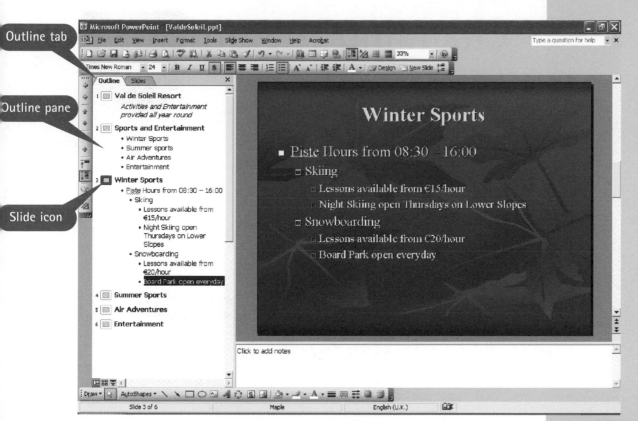

Figure 2.8: Moving text lines around

The text should have moved down the slide. You can move text from one slide to another in the same way.

- Click to the left of **Snowboarding**. Everything in this paragraph will automatically be selected.

- Drag downwards to put the text into the slide for **Summer Sports**.

- You don't really want it there, so click Undo. The Undo button is on the Standard toolbar at the top of your screen.

- You may want to enlarge some of the titles and text to fit the slides better.

Changing the order of slides

 Try moving Slide 4, **Summer Sports** below Slide 5, **Air Adventures.** (Hint: Click and drag the **Slide 4** icon.)

Click **Undo.**

Checking your presentation

You can view your progress so far. Look at it first in **Slide Sorter** view.

 Click the **Slide Sorter View** button at the bottom of the screen.

When you click the **Slide Show** button, the presentation starts at the selected slide (the one with a black border).

Click **Slide 1** to select it.

 Click the **Slide Show** button at the bottom of the screen.

Click or press the **Space** bar to move to the next slide. (Pressing the **Backspace** key goes back one slide. Remember you can exit your presentation at any time by pressing the **Esc** key.)

Take a break!

 Save your work using the **Save** icon.

Close the presentation.

Chapter **3**
Applying Designs

Now you're ready to think more about the overall appearance of your slides. Some slides may need a brighter background than others to increase their impact, or you may want to change the design template. Whatever your ideas, **PowerPoint** has many functions for customising the appearance of your slides.

Changing the Design Template

▶ Select File, Open to open the file named ValdeSoleil.ppt.

▶ Select Format, Slide Design... from the menu.

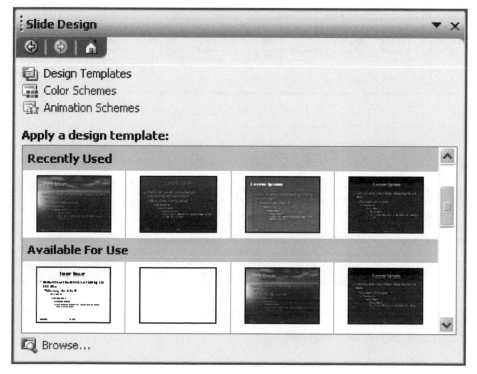

Figure 3.1: Selecting a new Design Template

Click the **Pixel.pot** design. You will notice that the **Maple.pot** design is the one you chose when you first began your project.

Note:

In some **PowerPoint** designs, the **Title** slide has a graphic which is not displayed on the other slides.

Changing the Slide Colour Scheme

With any slide selected, select the **Colour Schemes** option at the top of the **Slide Design** pane.

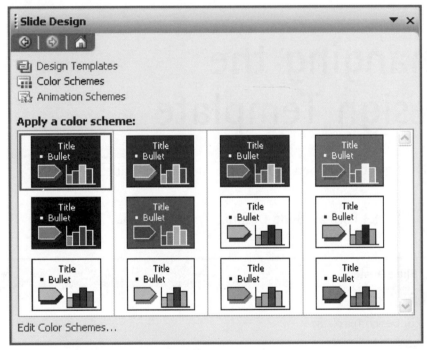

Figure 3.2: Changing the slide colour scheme

Select the top left design.

Tip:

This changes the colour scheme in all the slides. To change just the selected slide, click the down-arrow to the right of the scheme and select **Apply to selected slides**.

You can also try adding themed animation sequences using the **Animation Schemes** option.

Close the Slide Design pane.

Tip:

If the Slide Design pane is not visible, select **Format Slide Design...** from the Main menu bar.

Changing the background styles and colours

It is possible to change the styles and colours of the backgrounds in your slides without making any changes to the text colours or designs.

 Select Slide 2.

 Hold down **Shift** on the keyboard and select slide **6** to highlight all except the first slide.

 Choose **Format, Background...** from the menu bar.

 Now click the small down-arrow inside the **Background** fill box.

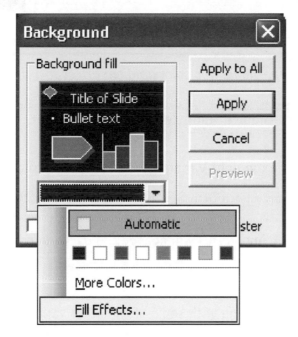

Figure 3.3: Changing the slide background

 Click **Fill Effects...** from the drop-down menu.

Figure 3.4: Applying a One color gradient effect to a slide background

 With the **Gradient** tab selected, click **One Color**.

 Select the top right **Variant** of the **Horizontal** Shading style. Click **OK**.

 Now click **Apply**. This will change the background on just the selected slides because they were selected earlier.

 Try experimenting with some of the other various settings in the **Fill Effects** window such as the **Colors** and **Shading Styles** available.

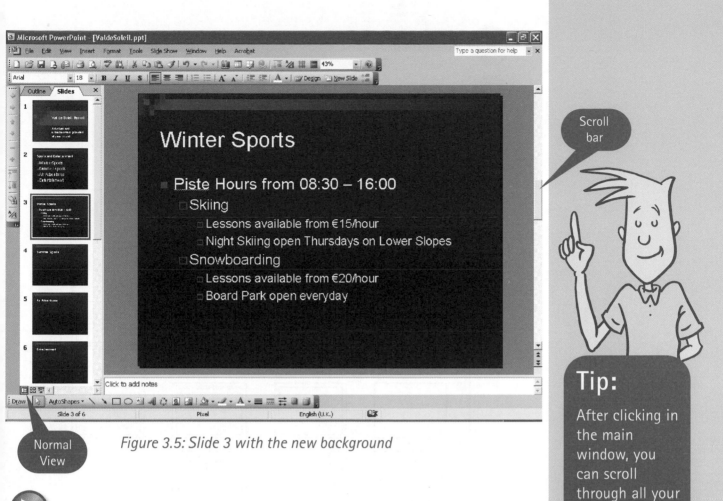

Figure 3.5: Slide 3 with the new background

Click the **Normal View** button.

You can also add textures or patterns to your slides in the same way by clicking on the **Texture** or **Pattern** tabs. (See Figure 3.4).

If you have a picture of your own that you would like to see as a background for your slide, you can add it by selecting the **Picture** tab. Then click **Select Picture** and find the picture you want to insert.

Changing the layout of a slide

PowerPoint allows you to choose between a number of layouts for each slide. Some layouts are suitable for slides with bullet points, others for slides which will include clip art or photographs, and others for slides showing charts or graphs.

Tip:

After clicking in the main window, you can scroll through all your slides using the scroll bar or the wheel on your mouse if you have one.

Tip:

It is important to select the correct layout for a slide before you add any objects. An **object** is usually a picture or chart.

▶ In **Normal** View, select the fourth slide titled **Summer Sports**.

▶ To select a new layout choose **Format, Slide Layout...**

▶ Select the layout named **Title and 2-Column Text** as shown below. Close the **Slide Layout** pane.

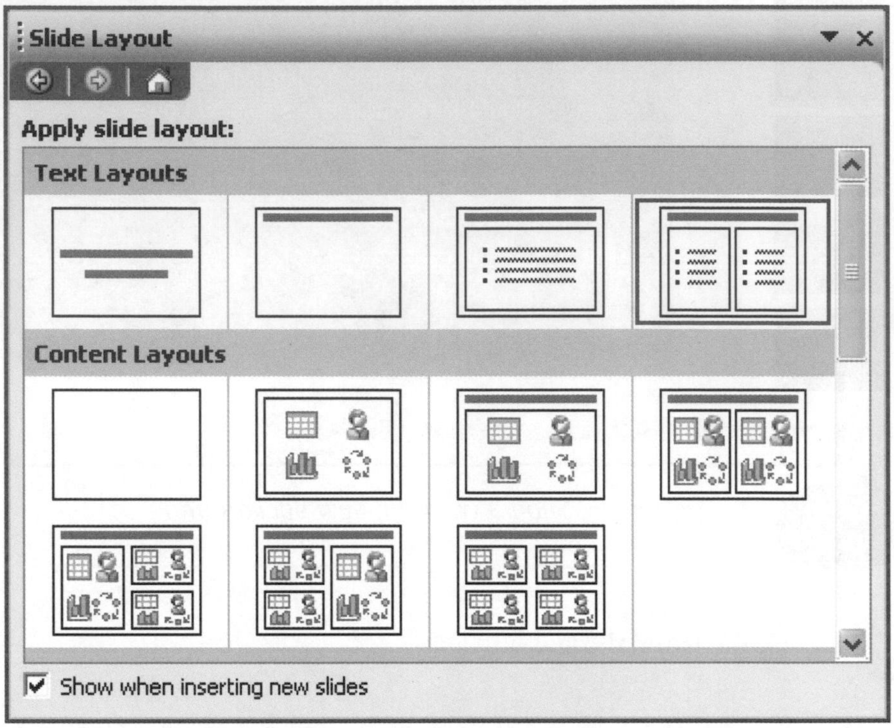

Figure 3.6: Selecting a new layout

▶ On the slide, enter the text as shown below.

Your slide should look like this.

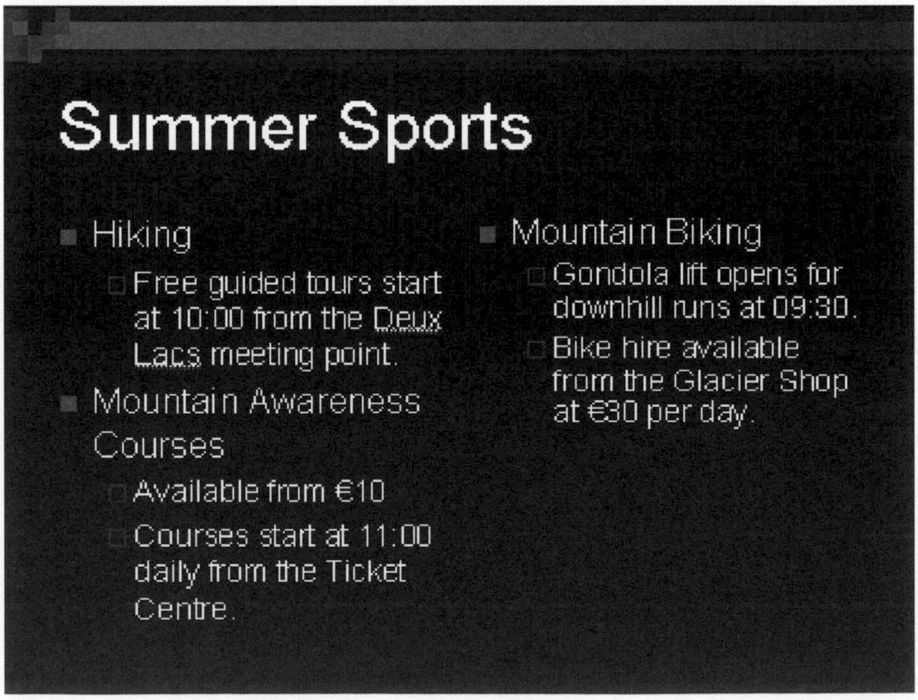

Figure 3.7: Column Text

If your text is smaller than in Figure 3.7, make it bigger by selecting it and clicking the Increase Font Size button. ———————

Choosing a layout to include Clip Art

The fifth slide will have a picture as well as text, so first you must change its layout.

 Select the fifth slide titled **Air Adventures**.

 Click **Format, Slide Layout...**

 Under **Other Layouts**, select the layout named **Title, Clip Art and Text** as shown below. Close the **Slide Layout** pane.

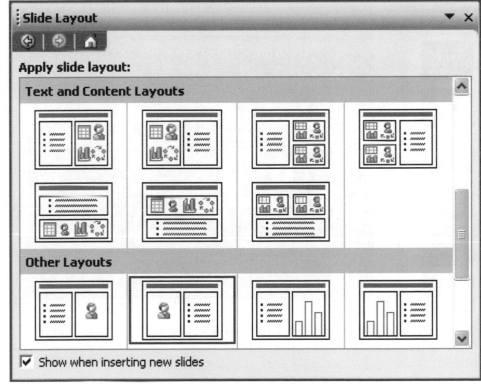

Figure 3.8: Text & Clip Art Layout

You will learn how to use Clip Art in the next chapter.

 Save and close your presentation.

Chapter 4
Adding Objects

You can add pictures, scanned photographs or cartoons to your slides. You can even put in graphs and charts.

 If it is not already on screen, open the presentation called ValdeSoleil.ppt.

 Click the fifth slide or scroll down to view the **Air Adventures** slide.

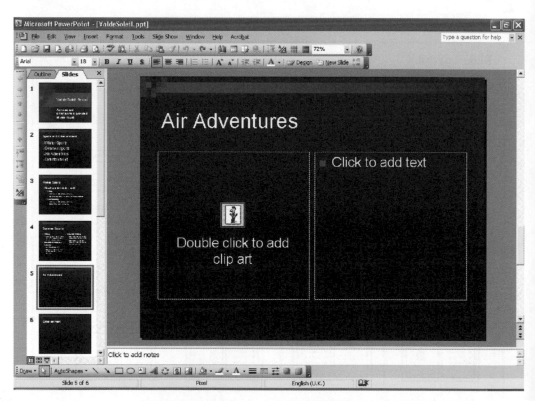

Figure 4.1: Slide 5 in Slide view

 Click where indicated to add text and type **Activities Available:**. Press **Enter**.

 Press the **Tab** key to demote the bullet. Add the sub-points: Parascending, Hot Air Ballooning and Hang-gliding.

 Increase the font size to fit the width of the text frame.

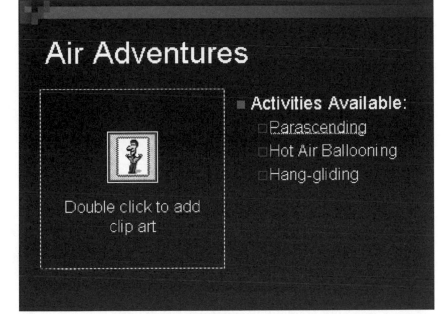

Figure 4.2: The fifth slide

Inserting a Clip Art image

You may have a CD with some clip art you can use. Clip art is simply a collection of pictures and drawings that have been drawn by professional artists and collected together for other people to use. PowerPoint comes with a small collection of clip art.

 Double-click where shown (on the **Clip Art Placeholder**) to add a clip art image.

 In the **Search text:** box type **Hot Air Balloon**. Click Search.

 Choose a good clip or try finding one on the Internet and importing it into PowerPoint.

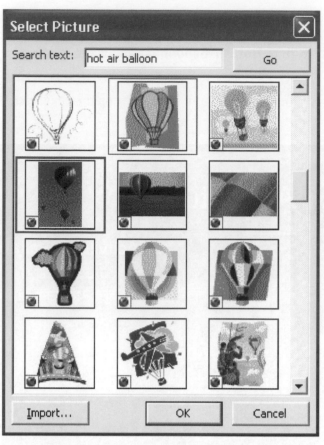

Figure 4.3: Choosing a Clip Art image

Click **OK** to place your clip art when you have made your selection.

Note:

The range of clip art available with the **PowerPoint** package is fairly narrow. You may also have a slightly different selection of pictures to choose from. A good place to find clip art pictures is on the Internet on Microsoft's On-Line Clip Art Gallery. You can get to this by going to **Insert, Picture, Clip Art...** and clicking the Clips Online link.

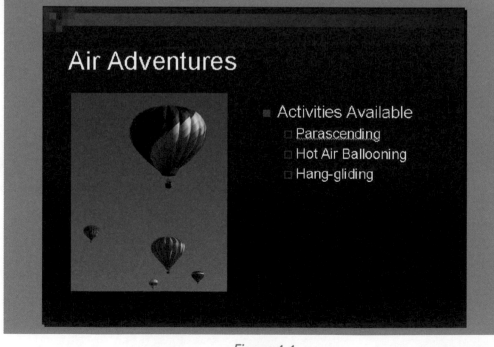

Figure 4.4

Handles

 Note the little squares surrounding the graphic (picture). These are called handles. When the handles are visible, the graphic is selected.

 Click away from the graphic and the handles disappear.

 Click anywhere inside the graphic and the handles will be visible again.

Changing the size of the graphic

You can make the graphic bigger or smaller without changing its proportions by dragging any of the corner handles.

 Make sure the graphic is selected so that the handles are visible.

 Move the pointer over the middle left handle until it is shaped like a horizontal two-headed arrow.

 Click and hold down the left mouse button. The pointer changes to a cross-hair.

 Drag outwards. A dotted rectangle shows how big the graphic will be when you release the mouse button. When it is about 1cm wider, release the button.

 Save your work so far.

Slide 6 could be created in a similar way. You can complete Slide 6 on your own if you have time, putting in some information about local entertainment and maybe some suitable clip art.

Adding a chart

Next, add a new slide to put a graph on.

Click the Slide Sorter View button in the bottom left of your screen.

Select the final slide by clicking on it.

Add a new slide by one of the following methods: click the New Slide icon, *or* use the menu option Insert, New Slide...

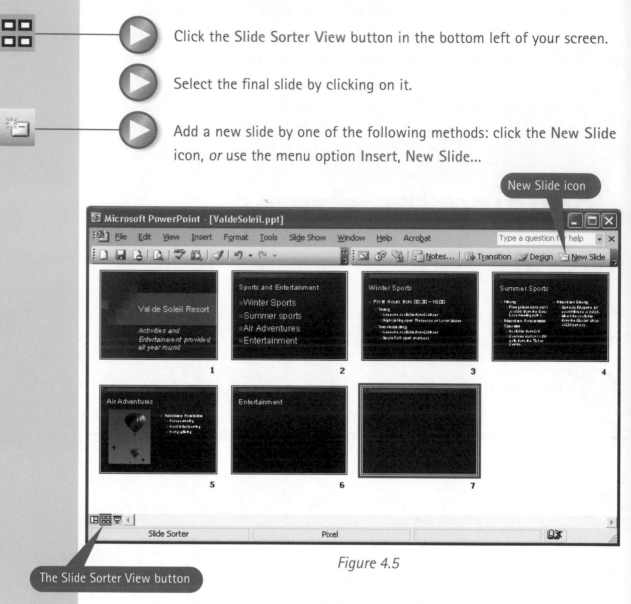

Figure 4.5

On this new slide you are going to create a chart to show the average temperatures throughout the year in the resort.

If the Slide Layout pane is not visible, select View, Task Pane from the Main menu.

Under Other Layouts at the bottom of this pane, select the last layout called Title and Chart.

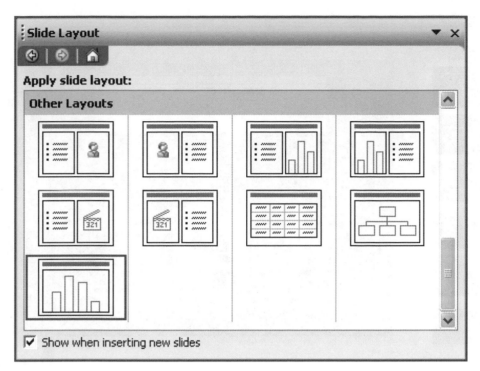

Figure 4.6: The Title and Chart layout

▶ Close the **Slide Layout** pane.

▶ With the new slide selected, click the **Normal View** button. ──────────────── 🔲

Now you are ready to begin making your chart.

▶ Double-click the chart placeholder that **PowerPoint** has created on the slide.

You will then see a small spreadsheet like you would see in Microsoft Excel. Notice that some of the icons on the **Standard** toolbar have changed.

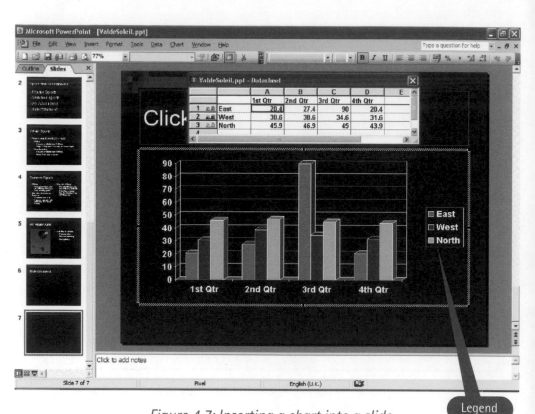

Figure 4.7: Inserting a chart into a slide

To make your chart you need to add your own information into the table.

 Click once in the cell labelled **East**.

 Now begin typing **Average Temperature**. This will replace **East**.

Double-click the border between the second grey column header and the column header marked A. This will increase the column width.

Drag the borders to resize columns

Val de Soleil.ppt - Datasheet		A	B	C	D
		1st Qtr	2nd Qtr	3rd Qtr	4th Qtr
1	Average Temperature	20.4	27.4	90	
2	West	30.6	38.6	34.6	
3	North	45.9	46.9	45	
4					

Figure 4.8: Widening columns

Replace 1st Qtr, 2nd Qtr… etc with 12 new column headings: Jan, Feb, Mar, Apr, May, Jun, Jul, Aug, Sep, Oct, Nov, Dec.

 You may need to make the datasheet wider and reduce the width of the columns by dragging the border between the grey Column Headers.

 Delete rows 2 and 3 by highlighting the grey Row Headers labelled 2 and 3 and pressing Delete on the keyboard.

 Key in the data as shown in Figure 4.9.

		A	B	C	D	E	F	G	H	I	J	K	L
		Jan	Feb	Mar	Apr	May	Jun	Jul	Aug	Sep	Oct	Nov	Dec
1	Average Temperature	-6	-2	1	6	18	26	28	30	24	14	7	-1
2													
3													
4													

Val de Soleil.ppt - Datasheet

Figure 4.9: Data in the datasheet

 Close the table by pressing the close icon. —————————

 Title your slide: Resort Temperatures.

The chart legend would look better if it were underneath the chart instead of next to it so we will move it.

 Double-click the legend to select the legend in the chart.

Now right-click the Legend and select Format Legend… from the pop-up menu.

Click the Placement tab and select Bottom from the list of options.

Click OK.

Click off the chart to view it properly and resize it to fit the page if necessary.

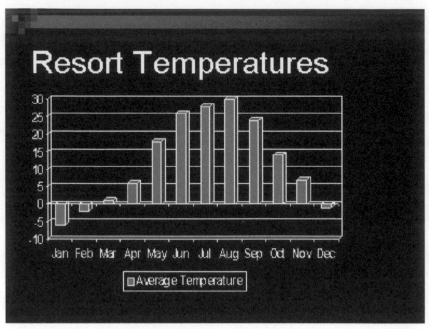

Figure 4.10: Slide featuring chart

Editing a chart

Suppose you have made a mistake in one of the figures or headings in the chart.

 Double-click the chart so that it is surrounded by a stripey border. Select **View, Datasheet** from the Main menu.

 Make any changes you want in the datasheet. The chart changes automatically.

 Click away from the datasheet and it will disappear.

Wrapping up

Click the **Slide Sorter View** button. This will let you see your presentation as a whole and organise your slides.

If you are happy, Save and Close your presentation.

Chapter 5
Special Effects

In this chapter you will be adding animation to the presentation. You can also add transition effects when each screen opens.

Multimedia objects and effects, such as pictures, animation and sounds help to keep the attention of your audience.

 Open the presentation ValdeSoleil.ppt.

 Select the Slide Sorter View and click the first slide. ⎯⎯⎯⎯⎯⎯⎯ ⊞

Viewing a slide show

Before you add any special effects to a show, it is a good idea to view it as it is. This helps you to build a picture in your mind of what it needs to jazz it up a little.

 Click the Slide Show button beside the Slide Sorter View button. ⎯⎯⎯ ⬛

Val de Soleil Resort

*Activities and
Entertainment provided all
year round*

Figure 5.1: Slide one in Slide Show view

▶ Click the mouse to change to the next slide.

▶ Keep going until **PowerPoint** returns you to the **Slide Sorter** view.

Adding slide transitions

Transitions change the way a slide opens. You can make the next slide open like a blind or a curtain, for example.

You will notice that in **Slide Sorter** view a new **Slide Sorter** toolbar appears somewhere on the screen. This has all the tools for adding transitions and effects to your slides.

Figure 5.2: The Slide Sorter toolbar

▶ With **Slide 1** selected, click the **Transition** button on the toolbar.

A Slide Transition pane opens:

Figure 5.3: Selecting a Slide Transition

Scroll down the list of different transitions and select Fade Through Black. This will make the first screen fade in from a black background like a television when you turn it on.

You can also change the speed at which the transition occurs. In most cases, Fast works well. Try experimenting!

You will notice a small icon appear underneath the slide. This represents a transition action on that slide.

View your changes by clicking the Slide Show button at the bottom of this pane. You will notice that the first slide now subtly fades in.

Tip:

If you click the right-hand mouse button while you are viewing your show, you can select **End Show** to stop it, or you can simply press the **Esc** key.

▶ Play

You can also view your slides in the Slide Sorter view by clicking the Play button in the Slide Transition window.

Adding transitions to multiple slides

You can apply a transition to more than one slide but not all by selecting them first, using the Shift key.

To add another transition to all the rest of the slides:

 Make sure that you are in Slide Sorter View.

Click Slide 2 and then hold down the Shift key.

 With the Shift key still pressed, click slide 7.

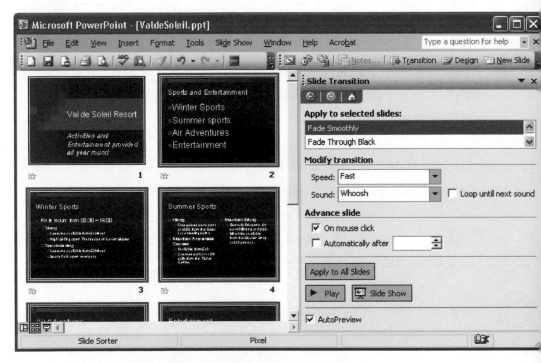

Figure 5.4: Selecting multiple slides

 Choose the **Fade Smoothly** transition.

 Click the **Slide Show** button to view the presentation. End the show when you have finished viewing.

Adding Sounds

You can add a sound to accompany the transition. For example if you have a slide that pops in from one side, you could put a 'whoosh' sound in there.

 With the **Slide Transition** window open, choose a suitable sound to accompany the slide from the Modify Transition section.

 Experiment with some different sounds.

Close the **Slide Transition** window.

Adding special effects to text

PowerPoint also allows you to add animation to objects such as clip art images, charts and bulleted lists.

Select slide 1 in **Normal** view.

Select Slide Show, **Animation Schemes...** from the menu.

Scroll down the list and select **Elegant**. Press the **Play** button to see the effects.

Tip:

If you wish to add a transition or sound to all the slides you need only click the **Apply to All Slides** button in the Slide Transition selection box.

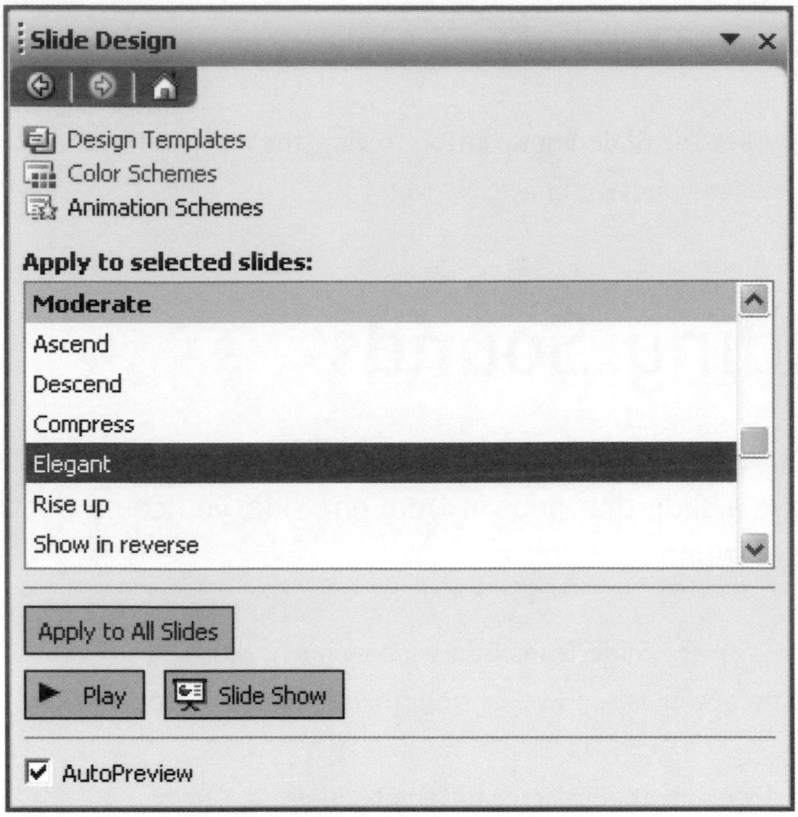

Figure 5.5: Adding animation schemes

 See your changes in Slide Show view. You have to click the mouse or press the Space bar to make the subtitle appear.

 Make the subtitle and title disappear one by one by pressing the Backspace key. Click the mouse to make them reappear.

 End the show and try out some of the other Text Preset Animations.

 Close the Slide Design window.

Using custom animation

PowerPoint will animate an object, such as a picture or chart, in the same way as it will text. You will need to use the Custom Animation... dialogue box.

 Look at Slide 1 in Normal View.

 Select Slide Show, Custom Animation...

You will notice that there are two animations associated with this slide and that one of them has a mouse icon next to it. This indicates that you would need to click the mouse to make it happen.

Figure 5.6: Using Custom Animation

 From the list, select the animation labelled 1, with the mouse icon next to it.

 Where it says Start: On Click in the Custom Animation window, change the setting to After Previous.

 Click the Play button to view the changes.

Now we will add some custom animation to the other slides.

 Select slide 2. Make sure that the Custom Animation window is open.

 Click anywhere over the Sports and Entertainment title on the slide.

 Click the Add Effect button.

 Select **Entrance, More Effects...** from the pop-up menu.

Choose **Fade** from the **Subtle** options. Click **OK**.

Change the **On Click** property to **With Previous** to make the slide title come on automatically.

Try double-clicking on the animation you have just set up. A new **Custom** window full of more exciting options appears.

Experiment with some of the other slides.

Close the **Custom Animation** window.

Save your presentation.

The **Custom Animation** feature is more complicated than most other functions in **PowerPoint** and fun to try out.
The best way to find out more is to try building your own presentation and experiment with different transitions, effects and animations. Give it a try!

You have effectively finished your presentation now. If you were going to present this to an audience yourself you would be just about ready to go.

PowerPoint has other features that can make a presentation work more like an interactive web site. We'll be looking at those in the next chapter.

Chapter 6
Action Buttons

In this chapter you will learn how to add Action buttons to a presentation. This makes it interactive. People reading the information in the slides can choose what to look at next and when to look at it, very much in the same way as a web site works.

Many places such as city high streets and shopping centres have interactive information kiosks for you to visit and find out information.

We will turn the Val de Soleil slides into an interactive presentation so that the slides will link together in the following way:

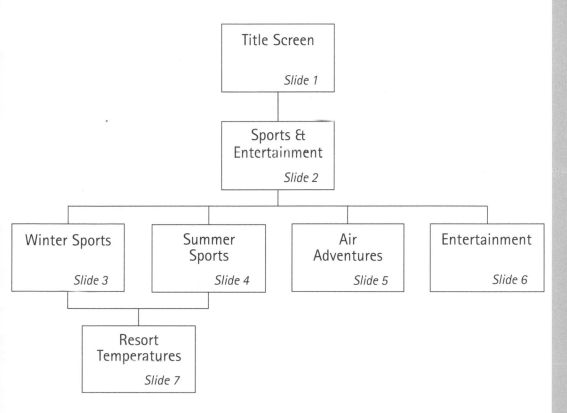

Figure 6.1: The slide menu structure

Open the ValdeSoleil.ppt presentation if it is not already open.

Adding Action Buttons

First you will add a set of buttons to go to each of the separate slides described in the slide text.

 Select the second slide.

 From the menu bar, select Slide Show, Action Buttons.

 Click the Forward or Next button to select it.

Figure 6.2: Adding an Action Button

 Move the cursor over the right edge of the slide opposite Winter Sports. The cursor changes to a cross-hair. Hold down the mouse button while you drag out a small rectangle for the button.

The **Action Settings** window should automatically appear.

Figure 6.3: Action Settings

Click the drop-down arrow in the **Hyperlink to:** box and select **Slide...**

 In the **Hyperlink to Slide** window select **Winter Sports** as the slide to link that button to and click **OK**.

Figure 6.4

Click **OK** again.

Click the **Slide Show** button in the bottom left of the screen to view your show and test the button.

Figure 6.5: Testing your new button

You should see the mouse pointer change into a small hand when it is over a button.

Press **Esc** to end the show.

 Reselect the second slide and create another **Action Button** opposite **Summer Sports**.

Link the slide to the **Summer Sports** slide in the same way as you made the hyperlink for the first button.

Figure 6.6: Adding Hyperlinks

Create 2 more buttons for the **Air Adventure** and **Entertainment** headings.

Figure 6.7

You can line up all your buttons and make them exactly the same size.

Keep your finger on the **Shift** key while you select all the buttons.

Select **Format, Autoshape** from the Main menu.

With the **Size** tab clicked, make each button a suitable size, say **Height 1.8, Width 3.5cm**.

Click the **Position** tab and enter a value for **Horizontal**, say 21cm, from **Top Left Corner**.

Save the presentation.

Adding a Home button

 Make sure that the Sports and Entertainment slide is still selected. We need to add a Home button to take the user back to the first slide.

 From the menu select Slide Show, Action buttons and add a Home button to the bottom right corner of the slide underneath the 4 other buttons.

 You should see that it is already hyperlinked to the First Slide. This is fine so click OK.

 Test the button.

Figure 6.8: Testing the new Home button goes back to Slide 1

Adding a Return button

Now we need to add buttons to slides 3 to 6 to go back to the Sports and Entertainment slide where all the option buttons are.

According to the menu structure diagram in Figure 6.1, another button needs to be added to slide 7 to go back to either the Winter Sports slide or the Summer Sports slide.

 Select the Winter Sports slide.

 Click Slide Show, Action Buttons from the menu.

 Select the Return button and drag out a rectangle in the bottom right of the slide.

 Click OK on the Action Settings window to confirm going back to the Last Slide Viewed.

Copying a button

 Select the new Return button and click the Copy button on the toolbar.

Now select Slide 4.

 Click Paste. A copy of the Return button should appear in the same position as it was on the original slide.

Paste another copy onto each of the remaining slides.

Your slides should now look like this:

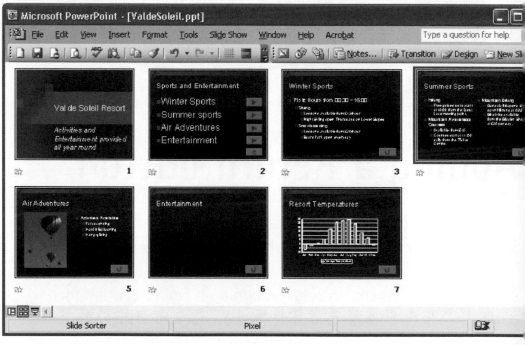

Figure 6.9

You now need to add 2 final buttons to the Winter and Summer Sports slides. These will go to the Resort Temperatures slide.

 Select Slide 3.

 Add a **Custom Action Button** just above the **Return** button on the slide.

 Click **Hyperlink to:** and select **Slide...**

 Choose the **Resort Temperatures** slide and click **OK**.

Figure 6.10

 Click **OK** again.

Adding text to a button

Some text needs to be added to this button instead of using one of the buttons with a graphic already on it.

 Right-click the new button and click **Add Text**.

Adding special characters

We need to add degrees Centigrade (°C) to the button. To do this, the degree symbol needs to be added.

 Click **Insert, Symbol** from the menu.

 Use the **Font:** menu to find a character font such as **Zapf** or **Wingdings** on your computer.

Figure 6.11: Adding a degree sign

Select the **Degree Sign** and click **Insert**.

Close the **Symbol** window.

Add a capital '**C**' to the degree sign in the button and enlarge the font to fill the shape.

Figure 6.12

Copy and paste the button to **Slide 4**.

Save your work.

Test your presentation.

*Chapter **7***
Slide Master

The Slide Master is used for adding text and graphics, often a company logo and slogan. These additions will then be displayed on every slide in the presentation.

Any change you make to the Slide Master will be visible on all the other slides in your presentation.

In this presentation we need to add a logo for the ski resort in the top right hand corner of every slide. The best way to do this is by using the **Slide Master**.

 Open the ValdeSoleil.ppt presentation if it is not already open.

Using the Slide Master

 Select View, Master, **Slide** Master from the Main menu.

You will notice that there are 2 master slides showing in the left pane of the screen. The top one is for slides 2 to 7 and the 2nd one is for the Title slide since this has a slightly different appearance from the rest.

We need to add a logo to both of the master slides so that it appears on all of the slides in the presentation.

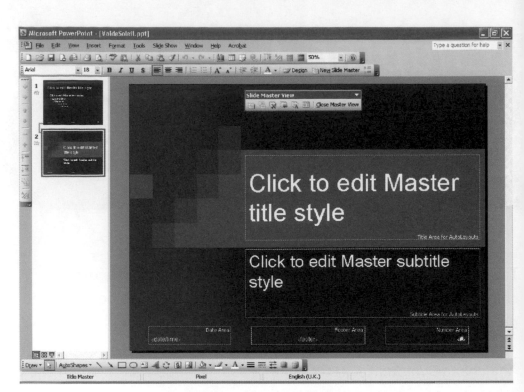

Figure 7.1: The Slide Master

 Select the first of the 2 masters.

A logo graphic is needed for this part. You can either use Clip Art or the Internet to find a suitable logo or you can download the one shown in this book from the Payne-Gallway web site.

 Click **Insert**, **Picture**, **From File...** from the Main menu.

Figure 7.2: Inserting an image

 Select your logo and click **Insert**.

Figure 7.3: The Slide Master

 Position the logo in the top right corner of the slide. Size it by dragging the bottom left-hand corner so that it is approximately the size shown in Figure 7.3.

 With the logo image still selected, click **Copy** on the toolbar.

 Select the 2nd master and click **Paste**. This will put a copy of the button in exactly the same place and size as on the other slides.

 Click the **Close Master View** button. ———

Slide Master View

☐ ☐ ☐ ☐ ☐ ☐ | **C**lose Master View

 Save your presentation.

Adding animation to buttons

You can 'add' animation to buttons in the same way as you do to other objects on the screen.

 Select slide 2.

 Hold down the **Ctrl** button and select the top 4 buttons.

 Select **Custom Animation...** from the **Slide Show** menu.

Click the **Add Effect** button.

Select **Entrance, More Effects...**

Figure 7.4: Adding effects

Choose **Ease In** and click **OK**.

Now select **With Previous** from the **Start:** option box.

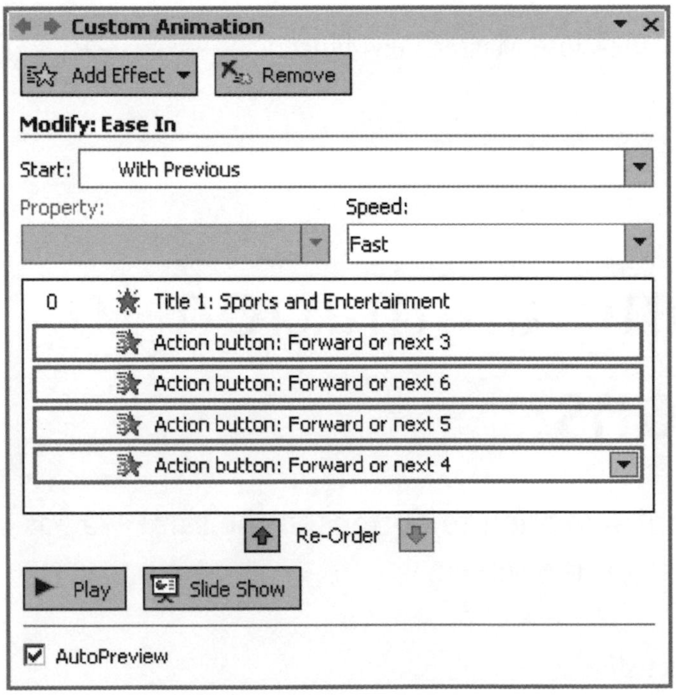

Figure 7.5: Adjusting timings

Try adding more animation to the rest of the buttons in the presentation as you wish.

Chapter 8
Testing

It is important to give your presentation a thorough testing to make sure that it works correctly throughout.

The best way to do this is to produce a structured test plan and follow it through making corrections as you find errors.

A table such as the one below will help with this:-

Test No.	Test	Method	Expected Result	Actual Result
1	Text animation on Slide 1	View show on Slide 1	Text automatically appears	
2	Change from Slide 1 to Slide 2	Click anywhere on Slide 1	Slide 2 appears	
3	Winter Sports button	Click on the Winter Sports button	The Winter Sports slide will appear	
4	Temperatures button	Click °C button	Resort Temperatures slide reappears	
5	Back button on Temperatures slide	Click Return button	Winter Sports slide reappears	
6	Return button on Winter Sports slide	Click Return button	Slide 2 reappears	
7	Etc..			

Figure 8.1: Test Plan

 Select **Slide 1** and choose **Slide Show, View Show** on the menu.

 Follow the test plan in Figure 8.1 and work through tests **1** to **5**. If you have done everything correctly up to now you should have no problems so far!

 Now perform test **6**.

You will find that the **Return** button on the **Winter Sports** slide does not in fact take you back to the **Sports and Entertainment** slide. This is an unexpected error and needs to be corrected.

 Press **Esc** to end the show.

 Make sure that the **Winter Sports** slide is selected.

 Right-click the **Return** button.

 Select **Action Settings...** from the pop-up menu.

 In the **Hyperlink to:** box select **Slide...**

Figure 8.2: Error corrections!

 Select the **Sports and Entertainment** slide as the linked slide. Click **OK** and **OK** again.

Press **F5** or click the **Slide Show** button to resume the slide show and re-test.

Try to think of some more tests you could conduct to make sure that *everything* works.

Tip:

Make sure to test:
Buttons
Animation Effects and Timing
Spelling, Punctuation and Grammar Content

Show Time!

Once you are sure that everything works and that all the text and spelling is correct, you are ready to launch your presentation and show it to your audience!

 Click the **Slide Show** button. ————————— 🖥

Hint:

You should find that the **Return** button on the **Summer Sports** slide has the same problem if you press the **Resort Temperature** button on that slide first!

In this particular presentation, users will probably use the buttons to navigate around the presentation themselves. However, if you have designed a presentation that you intend to give yourself, there are some options which you may find useful.

 Once in **Slide Show** mode, **right–click** the mouse and a small menu will appear.

<u>N</u>ext
Previous
Last <u>V</u>iewed
<u>G</u>o to Slide ▶
Custom Sho<u>w</u> ▶
S<u>c</u>reen ▶
P<u>o</u>inter Options ▶
<u>H</u>elp
Pau<u>s</u>e
<u>E</u>nd Show

Figure 8.3: Displaying the shortcut menu

Navigating your way around a presentation

To find your way around a presentation you can click the **Next** and **Previous** options on the pop-up menu. This will take you to either the next or previous step in the presentation.

If you want to move directly to a particular slide, click **Go** on the menu. This will bring up another menu in which you select **By Title**. Try going to the **Summer Sports** slide.

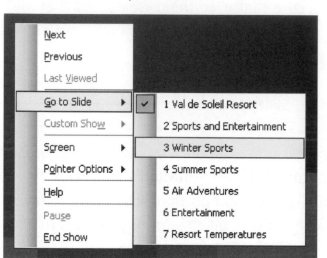

Figure 8.4: Navigation options

Exit from the show by right-clicking the screen and selecting **End Show**.

Help!

 Clicking the **Help** option on the pop-up menu offers you a list of useful shortcuts and commands which you can use in a presentation.

Slide Show Help

During the slide show:

'N', left click, space, right or down arrow, enter, or page down	Advance to the next slide
'P', backspace, left or up arrow, or page up	Return to the previous slide
Number followed by Enter	Go to that slide
'B' or '.'	Blacks/Unblacks the screen
'W' or ','	Whites/Unwhites the screen
'A' or '='	Show/Hide the arrow pointer
'S' or '+'	Stop/Restart automatic show
Esc, Ctrl+Break, or '-'	End slide show
'E'	Erase drawing on screen
'H'	Go to hidden slide
'T'	Rehearse - Use new time
'O'	Rehearse - Use original time
'M'	Rehearse - Advance on mouse click
Hold both buttons down for 2 secs.	Return to first slide
Ctrl+P	Change pointer to pen
Ctrl+A	Change pointer to arrow
Ctrl+E	Change pointer to eraser
Ctrl+H	Hide pointer and button
Ctrl+U	Automatically show/hide arrow
Right mouse click	Popup menu/Previous slide
Ctrl+S	All Slides dialog
Ctrl+T	View task bar
Ctrl+M	Show/Hide ink markup

OK

Figure 8.5: Useful commands

 Exit from the show by right-clicking the screen and selecting **End Show**.

Printing your slides

It is often convenient to print several slides to a page. You can use these as documentation or to hand out to an audience. There are several printing options available to choose from.

 From the menu select **File, Print...**

Figure 8.6: Printing slides

Select **Handouts** from the **Print what:** option box.

Choose your preferred number of slides per page and click **OK**.

Tips on setting up

If you are projecting the presentation onto a wall or projector screen, you can set up the computer screen in front of you so you can see it and have the audience watching the screen behind you. Make sure the slides are readable from all seats in the room.

Rehearsals

It is a good idea to rehearse a show on your own or with your group. This will help you to time the length of the presentation and remember what you are supposed to say.

Even a quick 5-minute rehearsal can make the difference between a poor presentation and a smooth, well-timed and polished performance.

You could try rehearsing in front of a small group of friends or family to help you get used to having an audience.

Check the hardware

Arrive early to give your presentation because you need time to check the hardware. Check that you know how to operate it and that it is all working correctly.

Facing the audience

When delivering your presentation it is best not to look at the screen too often. This breaks the eye contact you will have with your audience.

- Always look at the audience and maintain **good eye contact** with them.
- **Speak clearly** and don't rush.
- Be **enthusiastic**. Look as though you are really enjoying giving this presentation, even if you aren't!

Audience Interaction

To keep the attention of the audience it is often a good idea to ask them simple questions about your presentation. Test their knowledge before you tell them the answer.
Another way to keep the audience involved is to provide handouts. But don't give out long handouts just before you start speaking, or people will read the handouts instead of listening to you. Plan carefully what you need to give them and when.

Kiosk presentations

You may be planning to give a live presentation using a computer or an overhead projector. Another option is to create a self-running presentation that people can view at a kiosk. These are often found in shopping malls and entertainment complexes. You may decide to design an automatic, self-running presentation to run in the school entrance area or in a computer lab on a Parents' Day, for example.

With any of the slides selected, select Slide Show, Slide Transition from the Main menu.

The Slide Transition pane appears.

Figure 8.7

You can add your own timings to slides which will automatically display each slide for a set amount of time.

 From the Advance slide options click Automatically after. Select 5-second intervals. Click Apply to All.

This will now automatically flick through the slides in your show every 5 seconds. What you need to do is loop the presentation so that when it has finished, it starts again at the beginning.

 Click the Slide Show option on the Main menu and select Set Up Show... from the submenu.

 From the Show type category, select Browsed at a kiosk (full screen) from the window. Click OK.

Figure 8.8: Looping your presentation

This option will automatically loop the presentation until you press **Esc**.

A more advanced way of setting timings is to click the **Rehearse Timings** button on the **Slide Sorter** toolbar.————————————

Click the **Rehearse Timings** button. The slide show starts, with a new Rehearsal toolbar showing.

This will record the moment you click the mouse to move on. You can then request PowerPoint to save these timings and use them for your kiosk presentation.

Give it a try!

Index